From Mr. Bondo's Unshared Life

poems by

James Cervantes

Cervantes, James.
  [Poems. Selections]
  From Mr. Bondo's Unshared Life / By James Cervantes.
      pages cm
  ISBN 978-0-9836668-4-4 (alk. paper)
  I. Title.
  PS3553.E78F76 2014
  811'.54--dc23
                              2013031093

ISBN 978-0-9836668-4-4

H\s
HAMILTON STONE EDITIONS

Acknowledgements

Boston Review:
"How special it is to live in a special place"; "The Law of Remarkable Resemblance"; "At eight or ten he came to know himself"; "Mr. Bondo is two people in the world"

Poetry Now:
"Does everyone wonder about the birds" & "Now it is morning, noon, and night"

Hamilton Stone Review:
"When Mr. Bondo awoke with his hair on fire" & "Hundreds of miles to the south, in the frying pan city"

Hinchas de Poesia #7
"Someone is rattling a cage"; "The Greek liquor"; "There's a way-station for everyone"; "Mr. Bondo sings the blues"

Special thanks to Jim Heavily for a helpful critical reading of the manuscript.

~

James Cervantes attended the writing programs at the University of Washington and the University of Iowa, where he completed his MFA in 1974. Previous books include The Year Is Approaching Snow, The Headlong Future, Changing the Subject, Temporary Meaning, and Sleepwalker's Songs: New & Selected Poems. He was editor of *Porch* and *The Salt River Review*, and is now Foreign Correspondent for *Hinchas de Poesia*. He lives in San Miguel de Allende.

Contents

A hummingbird hovers before him

Someone slips out from Mr. Bondo's skin /41
Somehow, he missed the major campaign /42
He smelled her sunscreen before he saw her /43
Does everyone wonder about the birds /44
She had to stop and call /45
As if /46
He notices the *Do not disturb* sign /47
Now it is morning, noon, and night /48
Where you nursed is where you'll decompose /50
This evening, Mr. Bondo makes stew /51
Time to stop lying to himself /52

The frying pan city

The unresolved music of windchimes /57
Hundreds of miles to the south, in the frying pan city /58
When the body gives up its water /59
Someone is rattling a cage /60
There is too much day /61
Mr. Bondo senses an ear to the ground /62
The Greek liquor /63
Sleep does not come easily /64
He stands before red, black, and ochre /65
Now he is the trees and shrubs /66
Bondo's friend has made a mess /67
Long shadows as the sun heads south /68
He would like to say that he is more /69

The Law of Remarkable Resemblance

How special it is to live in a special place,
one which is photographed by tourists
and included in packaged tours. Mr. Bondo
wishes he lived in such a place. Sitting
on his somewhat run-down porch, he'd be the envy
of those shaking their heads from a distance:
that shake which means "How lucky! I wish
that was me," and their list of bad choices
as their eyes pan above Mr. Bondo
to staggering heights of granite
rising from his heavily wooded yard.

He would leave his almost-antique chair
and calmly disappear into the forest
to surprise himself with some newly-found den,
hardly hearing the motors anymore
and taking unto himself the tang of pine and juniper,
a soft and musky forest floor,
an afternoon of woods and pleasant footfall.
Mr. Bondo's photos of his special place
would be like those the tourists take,
and in which he provides a human scale.

*

At eight or ten he came to know himself
sitting on a window ledge, lost in the envelope
of a panorama, then a tunnel
in the air to the coast.

"Boy!" his mother yelled, and Mr. Bondo
lost his balance, grunting
like an animal phrasing a question.

Later, when window and view were one,
he'd forget the window seat
upon which he sat, and that he was looking
through the bay window, over the rooftops,
at cypress leaning from the sea.

These days, he sometimes
holds a window, steps through it
and forgets it
because he knows the way back.

He was that way with a person once.
She lives over there, like a view
from her window, and Mr. Bondo waves.

*

Over coffee, he gave in or gave up
in a paragraph about the fracas
in the Gaza strip. He couldn't finish the sentence
on a murderer. He didn't want to know
who was missing. He turned, instead,
to the bird named "Transformer"
which flew unexpectedly into his life: small,
metallic "Transformer," who'd grown
and softened, and whose feathers
were now parrot-colored ribbons
that twirled around a Maypole bird,
Mr. Bondo being ribbons and air,
common gaiety, an old story
he was so full of that spring
whirled within him, a kiss of wings.

*

The *Law of Remarkable Resemblance*
was born this good day, when Mr. Bondo decided
the world does not run on wires, or waves, or particles.
It runs, instead, on chains of tiny mirrors
that face each other like half-opened wings.
Excited resemblance finds itself
over and over in the face of each mirror
and spreads the word to its reflections.
They might, Bondo mused, be influenced
by an observer, so he looks over the shoulder
of a resemblance and is instantly included.

*

Mr. Bondo confesses that he is whole,
that he is the same as leaf or star,
that he is President and trembling on death row,
is the music made by one man
and the noise made by every music,
known only as random data
of the person who means most to him,
that the words "hope" and "wish" almost
make him cry in the mightiest bookstores
in the largest malls because they are
weak words, black on so many white pages,
his only desire – yes, "desire" is the same
as "wish" – to wake the very next morning
to a mockingbird that is wired
to learn the song of every bird
flying within its world, and to hear that
personally performed for Mr. Bondo
as part of his blessed wholeness.

*

He thinks you must divorce the gift
from the giver. Just as when his spirit-bird
(so-called in his diary) flew in out of the blue
as a tiny, delta-shaped craft (also confessed
as such in the diary) and inspired fear
in him, then joy as the thing transformed
into long, sinewy wings
that flapped like heartbeats, flight
coursing within Mr. Bondo's veins.

Songster was around for quite some time
and he flew with it, though unaccustomed
to such lift at night. In his flying,
Mr. Bondo did not notice an absence.
Stilled at last, he knew why his hands
and arms resisted his desk, why his chest rose
then fell so heavily, and why, in silence,
he could make song that neither practice
nor awkward instrument could provide.

*

Seldom dreamless, Mr. Bondo is disturbed
he cannot name the cast of last night's dreams,
as if, without names, the dreams did not exist.
He, who has had John F. Kennedy hold his hand
on a small ramp leading to a Lear jet, who ate
crumbs offered by Mao Tse-tung or the terra cotta
general in a secret prison beneath the Great Wall,
who made love to Joan of Arc, with her paisley shift
snagged on the buckles of his boots – he cannot,
for the life of him, mutter more than "she had long hair"
into his dream book, which is woefully inadequate
for those who measure life in details. Mr. Bondo
resigns himself to periodically hazy mornings
in which he wanders like a butterfly, unaware
of the word for morning glory, or jasmine,
or that sudden lull in morning breeze.

*

When Mr. Bondo awoke with his hair on fire,
he did the only thing he could do.

Having hung his drenched pajamas on a line,
he returned to find his bed unscathed,

no sign of frayed wires, no smoldering butts,
no ozone from a possible visitation.

Bondo meditated beneath his frizzy hair
until he was lost in the cobalt blue

of a mountain photo taken years ago, a puff
of white cloud to the right and above the peak

in late afternoon, when he'd forgotten the hours
following skittery paths, speaking out loud

to bushy, Kaibab squirrels, so frank and open
with their stares. He remembered the hour

and how the sun would be setting if he didn't
begin his descent. Quickly now,

and never mind the slipping.

*

Night after night, he digs deeply
in his yard for the golden helmet
buried somewhere near the base
of a monolithic boulder. Coronado
chose well, as the earth is soft
and there are no rocks save the giant one.

The summer nights wear the map down
to wet tissue, and Bondo is apprehensive
until he realizes he's dug the "X" so deep
he'll never lose his way. Three angels,
predictable in white chiffon and footless,
flutter their robes to cool his brow.

Surprised at the ease with which the earth
gives way, he places the first of three lilies
but cannot remove his hand from the pale
timekeeper, this harbinger revealed
by a peeling golden sheath, its roots
like hair buried more dead than alive.

*

His pal, the spirit bird, good old *Transformer*,
paid a visit in disguise. There was a dailiness
about the way they met the challenge, digging out
the truck while keeping the animal in its pen.
And there was no complaint about the mud
caked onto his arms and legs, making him
putty-colored and crazed like the varnish
on an Old Master which *Transformer*
lifted from the wall. He liked
losing his semblance that way,
unframed, peeling from the canvas
like shiny skin from a newly healed wound.
Translucent in the sun, the true picture
of himself floated to and fro, a child on a swing,
a leaf in spirit bird's disturbance of air.

*

This morning, Mr. Bondo believes
people in the airport look familiar.
That man with the mustache,
for example, is his brother before
he became clean-shaven. An ex-wife
holds a child who looks like her.
He wants to speak to her about this
but is not such a fool as to risk
his anonymity. He tells his mind
not to think the name of a woman
whose smile says "I-know-that-you-know."

So he continues breakfast
at the concourse cafe, seated
to watch arrivals and departures.
Mr. Bondo will not admit confusion,
and maintains a grip by checking
his ticket now and then, verifying
he is part of the departing stream.
Still, he desires a hug, as if
he were arriving. It would even do
to toss a gift at someone vanishing
down that telescope into a plane.

Practical Bondo recognizes
the absurdity of these thoughts
and, in near-panic, abandons breakfast
for a morning brandy and quick notation
in a small, spiral notebook, which he covers
with an awkward posture of his cigarette hand,
for he knows when he's given himself away
by an expression he can't hide.

*

Mr. Bondo is lost in a suburb
sprung up among cornfields where,
from a distance, every silo looks the same.
He wonders how many streets are named
after innumerable oaks, and how many times
they may cross streets beginning with *Stone*.

As dusk approaches, he points his rented car
toward a stream of lights a sudden rise
has revealed to him. He is relieved
that the highway's number is familiar
and that he knows which way to turn.

He will roost in the restaurant
with a border theme until he calls
and is found and retrieved. Men his age
seem interested in the TV's mute screens
and now and then stare at the acreage
of polished wood in front of their drinks.

He wonders if he's like them
and smiles to himself, though furtively,
when he thinks to ask the closest one
if he lives at something-oaks and
stone-something. That, surely, is a sign
that he's not like them. But Bondo is entranced
by the veins in his hands, which do not seem
as full as when he's home.

*

Anticipating a journey, Mr. Bondo gathers music
that will surround him in his car, measuring miles
in sixteenth notes, with pure, glass-edged sopranos
turned up high, wafting out an open window
to hang like mist on some buck's ear, and husky,
blues alto that weaves through the thump and whine
of tires on country asphalt. For the high plateau,
he grabs Vivaldi and Bach, because their notes
are like numberless sage dotting the ground
until, somewhere, a rock rolls off the edge
into the sky. Yes, he will have a great time
getting there, until he has to turn it off
and listen to the lights and signs humming
as they do when he's landed in the middle.

*

There's a way station for everyone,
one visited so often
that people assume you live there.

Such were his thoughts
dropping in at "The Wild Hare,"
where he asked again
if he might get his haircut.

No blame from Mr. Bondo
when he was told, again,
there'd be an opening
in his absence. Refusing
a menu was another
of his tags on home,
and accentuating "today" in
"What's the special *today*?"

There was "Hippy-Joe" at the bar,
not smoking and ordering tea,
and Bondo's usual mistake
of a familiar "Hi" to someone
as unanchored in this place
as he. Who would know

unless they followed him and saw
he never shopped for hardware
and was never bereft of toiletries?

Mr. Bondo likened himself
unto the weather of this place
occurring later down the road.

He is two people in the world

Summer settles in like a heavy guest
leaving too large an impression
in his favorite chair. It extends
beyond his arbitrary home
into a mountain retreat, where a man
fails to brush a leaf from his lover's hair
and Bondo shrugs as if he were that man
and the woman was forgotten for the leaf.

He looks at the trees along the street –
mountain ash no taller than one storey –
and senses a fullness without the sign
of opening leaves. The sky can carry
no more light and the mountains
cannot snag clouds. He will go now,
but return looking for that edge
when the town looks cut from air.

*

Today, Mr. Bondo will apologize
to strangers for uncommitted slights.
He will meditate upon his life
at unscheduled moments, like the brief pause
with coffee on a screened porch
before he piles into a van with relatives
and is taken shopping.

He finds a moment
in the mall with many fountains
where wishing pennies are running fish.
Mr. Bondo seems to bounce
off monogamous faces
wrapped in broadcast song.

"I'm sorry," Bondo says
to the first pair of bottomless eyes,
referring, the recipient assumes,
to the slight discomfort
from his too familiar stare. It is time,
he thinks, to buy something,
put it in a bag, and call it his.

*

His dog cannot sit still in the homes
of others and comes to check
Bondo's scent from time to time.

He is not so different from the dog.
He smells water, the lingering edge of coffee,
then something in the upholstery

or a ghost of body scent
that recalls the home of a dying man
who died trying to be family.

He wonders what airy paths
the dog must follow, and if they cross
or end somehow in the familiar,

or if the dog desires more
than human resolution and just visits
Mr. Bondo as a momentary link

before it bounds away on its broad path,
a black dog in the night sky
remembering star after star.

*

Mr. Bondo is two people in the world
this afternoon on the viny campus
and two people again at the grocery store.
He is maybe one person in the dog's
deep brown eyes, and nothing
to the desert milkweed
whose meager thirst he satisfies.

He thinks there might have been three
of him for his wife, possibly four
when he would leave for walks alone.
Absent one, zero on the keyboard,
untouched while fingers took
one order of letters into another.

In this mood, his friends multiply
into unknowns. One turns a smile
toward him and into his eyes
and he knows; one of several backs
walking away and he knows. But who
is that in a story in Chicago, driving

past what he thought was her hometown,
ignoring the signs held out for her, running
right through a cloud of details? Mr. Bondo
thinks of a crowd on a ship waving
to a waving crowd on shore, and how
easily he could be in both.

*

Yesterday, he tried to find shade
under a patio umbrella and realized
he was hiding from his own thoughts,
whispers from a hidden road
the other side of a man-high fence
where he'd been lost. But now
he's connected to a hot-air balloon
drifting partially along the flat horizon
and partially below the fence: there is that
which he can't see, and that which is
related but obscured by fences.
Mr. Bondo spelled it out because
he knew his missing hosts
were not metaphorically inclined
and had no time to waste, here
in the cornfield, or over there.

*

Enough of this, enough of that,
I'm up to here with it, never again,
not another minute, don't you dare . . .

Mr. Bondo's rant hung
because there was no "you"
and his dog, a Malamute,
stopped chasing its tail
and regarded him.

"Oof!" it said, and sat, lay,
then rolled over
to have its underbelly scratched.

Bondo's ears rang from the bark
but cooled somewhat from the wild
wind that scurried off into the dark. Why now

that train whistle in the distance?
Or the moon like a bloated actress
playing peek-a-boo with clouds
as if they were curtains? Evening dust

is different, he thought, as is
night jasmine from day, and pressed
his nose deeper into the screen
to catch the change as rain
swept in, passed by, then stayed.

*

He has taken to hiding scents from himself:
the hand cleanser, antiseptically sharp,
which takes him to a certain room; pine nuts,
which open him up to make space for a forest;
a certain lotion that brings him empty hands.

Paper, fresh from the printer, and old paper
that slowly decomposes and takes him
to the libraries of his youth – those are alright.
Even the two pines in his yard, about which
he can do nothing, and whose transport ends
when he simply looks up at them.

No, he is out to import new scents,
perhaps ubiquitous furniture
with equatorial sap still present
in its wood, or a fresh coat of paint
on everything, or leaving the windows open
through four seasons, a year of sweeping
by the wind from all directions.

*

Business intrudes on Mr. Bondo's
sun-struck summer. He feels like an orange
waiting on water from frantic
little hands clawing into stubborn dirt
only inches from rock, crumpling
their little pails, mindful he might wither
before shouting *yellow*.

He feels like a tree without choice
on the western side of a hill,
there for the pleasantries of birds
and updrafts of winds, until the alarm
of afternoon and sunset, when it
must truly wake and burn again.

But it's simple, really,
to make marks where there was nothing before,
fill in the blanks with what is called for,
and then go from left to right
and up and down again, like a stream
where rocks still tumble in,
its banks receiving a flood
as Mr. Bondo does.

*

A person sits on the steps of a deck
that juts into the space between house and forest.

Clouds change and move quickly from southeast
to northwest, but much more quickly for this person, a man
who has just noticed himself sitting on the steps of the deck.

He has always looked up at the clouds, but now they change
at every glance. Distance is closing for him. His thoughts
are right here, sitting on the steps, witnessing.

Just like that, the swallow he has admired
for the last few minutes lands not three feet from him.

He almost breaks into tears, for he could be happy
witnessing or being the still part of clouds that move so fast

or swallows that see him, then don't.

*

Mr. Bondo sings the blues
with air-guitar and shadow-dances

with a rented horn.
He doesn't like his belly

full of blues and a heart
as empty as Kansas City

when that wind blows in
at 3 a.m. and sweeps streets

like long-legged woman
turning in her sleep.

Mr. Bondo sings the blues
to the Gulf of Mexico,

picks up shells to hear the chorus
from Houston to New Orleans,

licks salt from bricks,
drinks ocean from the fog -

man on the move, feeling
that outgoing tide

like long-legged woman
turning in her sleep.

*

The smell of another adheres to him.
Perfume and body. Opening the door
to the house causes the scent to snake
from the cotton coverlet through an arch
into the living room, then answer
sinuously to the open entryway.

There is no faint version of it.
Steam from a shower seems to release
hidden reservoirs to which
he contributes. Likewise the rush
of hot water into the washing machine,
and the pillows exhale it.

Later, he sniffs the sodden lumps
before the dryer thumps them
into wads he will not lay
his head upon. There is clarity
in blood to the brain after lying flat
upon material smells.

*

Early dog days. Yard work to be done
under the fireball
in dust that rises from the grass
and sifts down from leaves.

He does it mindlessly.
Why not? It's all push and shove,
swipe and pull. And afterwards,

after desiccated air has dried him,
he chances upon stars
glittering on the backs of his hands,

the microscopic salt
of his own water, his self-made sky
trailing up his wrists and forearms,
and he takes off his shirt

to see sky everywhere. How far away
from himself must he be
to know that under stars

there is only this.

A hummingbird hovers before him

Someone slips out from Mr. Bondo's skin
taking all that Mr. Bondo is
except for one gasp
and he

is the sliding door
that keeps behind glass
the terrace and garden,

      a balloon trailing its string, blossoms
      skittering across fallow ground.

People can be storm,
little whirlwinds
at revolving doors, or a perfumed wind
you didn't know you were waiting for.

      Braced against a gale force spring,
      do we saunter with Indian summer?

He doesn't know, nor does the other.

These are two men back to back
hoping to step into a stillness,

each with his answer to *Let go, Let go* . . .

*

Somehow, he missed the major campaign
in the Urals, and the one in the swamps
where those to the left and right of him
lost their lives. Likewise the beaches
where ads are filmed, and again
he cannot remember the names or faces
of those to the right or left.

Still, he mourns
those in peripheral vision
who could have been himself,
their noses and audible breath,
trunks and legs in the self-same
uniform invisible to him.

Khaki is the color of desert, or eucalyptus
with shadows of peeling bark, certain stones
exposed on mountain tops, or of some beaches.

Somehow he'd been spared
to think these things, to remember
emptiness when he tries
to bring back the names. "Ackelstrom!"
blurts in his mind, and he knows instantly
those are three men blurred together
before a colonel, or at a breakfast
where full plates are suddenly dumped into a bin.

It was so long ago. Even the ground
they wanted so much to be a part of
is overgrown and renamed, and the beaches . . .
Well, there is less to them, or more.

*

He smelled her sunscreen before he saw her,
and also her husband's tangy cologne
wafting through walnut and stunted pine.

"Excuse me," she says, pointing to a rock shelter,
"but do you know why we cannot enter?"
"Because," he lies, "they found a couple making love."
And the husband stoops and peers around the sign
which forbids all but park employees to enter.
Ich meine, er luegt. Aber vielleicht nicht.

Later, at his summer home, Bondo wakes
as the rooster in the east crows
and the rooster in the west answers
from across the meadow. Two elk
saunter from the forest, their racks aglow
in the rising sun, and he thinks of the couple,
how they never emerged from the shady side
of the cliff to join him as he climbed, sweating,
past stony rooms in full morning sun.

He imagines the man's pupils
dilating in the darkness, his new belief
in urgent, earthen beds, and the woman's scent
returning to the ruins, echoes of crow and dove.

* *Ich meine, er luegt. Aber vielleicht nicht.*: I think he lies, but
perhaps not.

*

Does everyone wonder about the birds
that come and go in the yard? Are those really
the same two doves every morning, the same grackles
arriving like a gang on vacation, the very same
hummingbird going eye-to-eye with a pair
of perfect, odorless blossoms that blink?

Or do they all strut, squawk, and stare
in the same way on any stage? He wonders
because he wishes a special usefulness
for himself and his yard: that he has planted
the right things for delight and sustenance
of birds, that his cats swoon and are paralyzed
by so much bounty, that his dog

merely cocks its head like Mr. Bondo
when a hummingbird hovers before him,
mesmerizing with its blur of wings, the black dwarves
of its eyes blinding him to the color of air that surrounds it.

*

She had to stop and call
from the playground's phone booth,
alarmed that the new moon
was not yet visible at dusk.

Perhaps it was location,
but her woman's face turned girlish,
swept blankly past him and looked up.
He looked where she looked
and there the mountains
bled darkness into darkening sky.

Why this fear over an absent moon
in the playground's phosphorescent glow
and with new stars in the east? Why
had she not mouthed words into the phone?

He looked out the car's window at her
and she, as still as the merry-go-round,
looked back at him. Where would they go,
what would they do, each alone, but together
like this, with no way to hurry the moon?

*

As if
after a long time,
the sun has not moved
but the shadow of bamboo palm
is sharper, the bedspread
and chest of drawers
with haloed edges, as when
photographs are hastily
superimposed,
grafted onto each other
to portray an ideal.

And, as if, after sundown,
he has not moved
but is six hundred miles
down the road, awake too long
and still too far away,
map on the seat
and lights turned on
for oncoming traffic
because he can see
this lost way in the dark.
He'll slow and halt
when a certain sign
turns off its lights.

*

He notices the *Do not disturb* sign
hanging on a doorknob down the hall. He knows
it's for the housekeepers, but can't help himself
and wonders if love might be more gentle
than he'd thought. The sign is not that different
from *Please stay on the path* and *Avoid stepping*
on the plants. Once he'd seen: *If you can't resist touching,*
please return object to its original location.

"No, I promise I won't knock," Bondo protests
to no one in particular, for in his mind he sees
a face resting on a pillow, lips slightly open,
the body's dew on the eyelids, the fingertips
of the right hand under the right cheek, and two
pale bands from rings that have been removed
from the second and third fingers. It's too easy
to stay on the path away from this person

he'll never meet, he thinks. Perhaps if he met her,
he could obey the signs, never touch
what she chooses to wear, never insist on a kiss
other than the one he blows from his hand. Mr. Bondo,
striding down the hallway, makes up such stories
for each wagging sign, and remembers to remove
dead blossoms and bank the roots of roses
when, at the foot of a door, he sees the wreck
and smear of dinner plates.

*

Now it is morning, noon, and night
and he feels free to talk to himself

about a small chunk of childhood
in the corner of the room, contemplate it

and even feel the raised letters
of its partial alphabet: the "A"

and the "B," and somewhere
a corresponding apple and ball.

He can talk of embossed yearbooks,
or envelopes with Eisenhower cancelled

by sine waves, which impart the motion
of a breezy flag to what was once

sufficient postage to carry love.
He speaks of the weightier years

as if they were an unsealed carton,
perhaps still added to, with some large

mistake sticking out, perhaps a foot
with nail polish glistening on the toes.

But the supposed leg and supposed torso
continue somewhere, and the face

is framed and on someone's desk.
All the while, he has eaten, taken a walk,

read a book, and done some shopping,
talking his way into the moment,

commenting that the man in the moon
is in the mirror, and that behind him

all of the named and unnamed stars
go on as questions and certainties

like a conversation in sleep.

*

Where you were nursed is where you'll decompose.
Mr. Bondo cannot find the question
for that answer. But there it is again,
this time at 58th and Broadway, undressed
and not even shivering, as it were, its origin
like an erasure on a blackboard.

At the party, the hostess is older than he.
Where you nursed is where you'll decompose
comes mid-sentence and mutes
what she says on the edge of her chair,
attentive, ready to rise and greet
a guest already halfway across the room.

We were so worried about you, said his mother,
We didn't know if you were back. Then, out
of some airy hollow fifteen hundred miles away,
from hours when she hadn't existed: *Did you
get married?* He wants to laugh in her face,
but he will not laugh in his mother's face.

He wants to turn his back on whoever says
Where you were nursed is where you'll decompose
because it comes when he is wakeful,
the voice bright in his ear, unlike filaments
of dream one walks into and through, ignorant
of their shimmering anchors slipping away.

50

*

This evening, Mr. Bondo makes stew,
a *boeuf bourguignonne* with good burgundy,
because it complements the smell of dead leaves,
those falling as they die, letting sunshine
hit the house from the east in November.

He will have to rake, but thinks he will wait
until the trees are bare, until the sun's
critical angle is significant and marked
transition occurs. He read of this
somewhere and will apply it to his life.

His neighbor is playing music outdoors,
tacking lights to his eaves. Smell of manure
for winter rye lingers, so Bondo goes inside
for the onion, bay leaf, thyme, the soupy mix
of tomato, oils, and beef. He sniffs and decides

there will be no tree this year, no fussing
with lights or the history of ornaments.
Fainter smells of carrot and mushroom
follow him around the house, piquant
green pepper, perhaps the water and salt.

*

Time to stop lying to himself.
It is never intent that takes him
here or there. Even now,
revisiting the bay of leaden water
spread beneath familiar hills,
home, that deep, round word,
slips off the tongue in his mind
under close gray skies.

Home, whose silly smile hovered
above the confluence of two rivers,
smiled as happily in a trailer
on dead-end gravel; the base
of a mountain and the whole
of its hundred-mile slide
down to high desert, easily
conned into *home*,

And cities, cities absurd
in their existence as map,
a maze of streets with names,
the homey intersections
of curb and manhole, a park
and the crease of a fold,
D-12, K-32, P-47, -
all of them embraced
because he is there.

"You are here,"
with a red mark and arrow,
because the universe is spherical
and its center is *you*. Even if

the flat circumference
includes some cork
and space beyond the frame,
there's always a store window
or windshield reflecting someone.

The frying pan city

The unresolved music of windchimes
persists in the afternoon,
always after the wind has passed
and without a beginning.

Be gone, stay, begin now,
wing, be gone, he hears them chime.
They stop before the pine says *hush,*
then they follow with *gone, now stay.*

Gone where, stay where, begin what,
he cannot ask, because *wing* chimes,
then *now* and *stay.* He is gone
before the pine is still, a wing now,

without a beginning, without a way.

*

Hundreds of miles to the south, in the frying pan city,
a large lens focuses the sun on those who scurry

from house to car. Mr. Bondo is heading there,
where channeled water flows into kidney-shaped lakes

and ponds like lungs without air. He is falling
past the shores of an old sea whose salt still glimmers

and whose shells are bowls full of sand. Cedar
and juniper have tipped their roots in; the piñon

gave up miles ago. His hand lets go of the wheel
on a curve whose tangent throws him

into the plump barrel of a cactus, arms up
into the sky. Hallelujah! The land

of lizard gods, snakes of dry belief.

*

When the body gives up its water,
white bracelets
form on the wrists, ankles,
neck, and highlight
bony points of the face.

When the soul gives up its water,
it gives one
last lick to the body
to savor its host, to taste
what is left of water.

*

Someone is rattling a cage,
someone is reading a newspaper,
someone is fighting a fire.

The weather is putting a damper
on everyone's summer plans
while peace talks fail: signs

of an age, smoke from a fire.
So the person reading turns a page,
the one rattling bites the bars.

*

There is too much day,
too much of the wrong light
seeping into the third eye
waking in someone's cloud of play.

As if unwanted children
had reduced the garden to dust,
kicked up desiccated leaves
as a kind of dead snow.

"It looked like a monkey,"
she said of the fetus,
"tubes and sacs of blood
moving like a beheaded snake."

But today's news is of holes
blasted through a young adult
who showed much promise,
and of strong light shining through them.

As if the cartoonist was right,
or the filmmaker who slows life
and death until both
are the same spherical window.

Not up there, in the arch
of a nave, but down here
where something has gnawed a hole
just above the kitchen floor.

*

Mr. Bondo senses an ear to the ground
that is not his
and so he lifts his head

with its warped halo
of cartilage, a green smudge
which the server will comment upon

later, when he orders the tea
he has not had in years, Lapsang-Souchong,
last ordered in Edinburgh

in the company of people with large pores
visible like the rhythm
of the amateur band, not exactly

oompah-pah, but close
enough to ruin a moment of
marriage renewal, of silent vows

shouted drunkenly, though sincerely
enough to be wearing berets, goatees,
and clothes of mourning.

*

The Greek liquor
goes down easily, clear
or milky. He prefers it
milky, with the magic of ice.

Someone always turns
on a barstool to ask,
"Why does it do that?"
But he can never
remember the catalyst.

Better to let mystery
hang over the bar, better
to swallow the kiss
and wonder tomorrow

why the woman slid on her back
down blue ice,
her lengthening hair
turning white on the mountain.

*

Sleep does not come easily
to him, but then it wins
like a broad blade flashing
through the dust of horses.

Moonlight on a dark stream,
hoot of an owl, splash
of a sleepless trout. Hand
on fin, Mr. Bondo goes

hunting in the waters
among silvery lights and eels
until his guide turns its only eye
toward him. It is human

and even has lashes. Bondo
knows the look of fear and hangs on
until they clear the surface
and he is tossed, flapping

sprays of water until
he is merely scattering dust
under setting moon and rising sun.

*

He stands before red, black, and ochre
handprints on cliff walls, close
to where water pools, anywhere the hand
extends from the mind to ask,
to make, to sign itself.

He covers them with his own hands.
The warm stone feels much like flesh
and its words are *It's just me.*

Mr. Bondo takes this home
and several hours disappear
under the great Aleppo pine.
Squatting, arms extended, palms up,
he understands the gesture.

Open and weaponless,
he further translates his hands as *no rock.*

With a branch from the pine,
he makes circles in the dirt
and gives them words: *I gave it away,
that's why it's not here, in my hands.*

*

Now he is the trees and shrubs
that look as if photographed,
meaning they are very still
and will remain so until
someone brushes them or
the waiting storm decides
it is time to saunter in.

The trees are Shamel ash
and the shrubs *juniperus*
and *justicia*, one with many
blades caught in the act,
and the other limply there,
but this in no way changes
what may or may not happen.

The storm is called monsoon
while the moon wanes yet again
in the Christian calendar year
of two thousand, which again
changes nothing in terms
of whether rain will fall
suddenly and quickly.

It's possible he will stay
when rain comes, and remain
stiffly in his limp clothes
like a flag on a pole, or run
into the house and rejoice
through a window, steady
houselight behind him, jagged
lightning on the other side.

*

Bondo's friend has made a mess
for someone to find, the new pistol
fired with meaning for the first and last time.

A switch that turns everything off,
its blast and silence are one in the same.
But that is just Bondo's conjecture.

One version of a family history is gone,
snuffed out, one version of Bondo
and of each and every friend.

And for the neighbors: That shot
no more than a shoe dropped.
Bondo suspects these are not original thoughts.

Only one version of his friend is gone.

*

Long shadows as the sun heads south
and a leaf drops as if on cue.

The newspaper is damp. Windows go down,
muffling music meant for him,

but he hears their weights rattle
in the frames of a war-time house.

Rain comes, of course, and the world
is outside-in. Staring at dripping ferns,

glistening moss, and the darkening mirror
of his street, he hears an edgy newsman

talk of death and battleships. The pictures
are right there, reflected in the window,

if he wanted to look at them, and the hole
in the battleship's side would just be

part of the window revealing a flowerbed,
if he happened to look that way.

*

He would like to say that he is more
than the letter he is writing
and perhaps prove that with
a blood-red seal, or a drop
of blood itself. The paper
already has a moist dimple
of sweat and the faint odor
of his tobacco. Perhaps a seed
from his favorite dying tree
in the envelope, a pinch of
acidic soil, the pressed blossom
of a midsummer rose?

So much to be carried
on the back of a mailman
through a neighborhood as seen
by a child on his first solo walk.
The invisible string that ties him
snaps one house away from home.
A mother hangs clothes, a father
mows the lawn. All of the houses
empty their children and he
follows their backs. Each house
could be a single stone, each
set edge to edge on grass.

So why send a sampler
of his life into a home
familiar only to another,
and otherwise just a shell
for a hermit crab laden
with a message? What's to prove
except that little feelers

must make an irritating noise
as they slide along pink
and pearl-gray walls. And once
in the perfect niche, does it
remember by sleeping always
with its eyes wide open?

He walks over dramas
on a beach: an empty bottle there,
a sodden receipt, and pink sandals
with broken thongs. Salt air
comes in like thick medicine
timed to waves, timed to his walk
until both lungs have their portion.
But machine time and broken thread
take over, a relative's talk
interrupted by broken sewing.
How does one resume a special stitch
without some tying? Things unsaid
must be like that: what is felt
is finished with uneven breath.

www.ingramcontent.com/pod-product-compliance
Lightning Source LLC
LaVergne TN
LVHW091209080426
835509LV00006B/902